CYPRUS

Compact Guide: Cyprus is the ultimate quick-reference guide to this popular destination. It tells you all you need to know about the island's attractions, from ancient legends to modern passions, idyllic sandy beaches to rugged peninsulas, dense forests to defiant castles and remote mountain monasteries to bustling cities.

This is one of almost 100 titles in *Insight Guides'* series of pocket-sized, easy-to-use guidebooks intended for the independent-minded traveller. *Compact Guides* are in essence travel encyclopedias in miniature, designed to be comprehensive yet portable, as well as up-to-date and authoritative.

D1413253

Star Attractions

An instant reference to some of Cyprus's most popular tourist attractions to help you on your way.

Nicosia p16

Kourion p42

Rock of Aphrodite p44

Paphos p46

Ayios Neophytos p52

s p57

Girne/Kyrenia p59

Güzelyurt p63

Buffavento Castle p67

Salamis p72

the balmy evenings are a delight. The summer climate on the Mesaoria plain, however, can be unpleasantly hot. Light, summer clothing is fine for the beach at all times of day but, even in July, take a sweatshirt on a trip into the mountains. The dry summer lasts into October, sometimes even November, but then suddenly, without an autumn interlude, the rainy season starts. Restaurants and most hotels close. Of the hotels that remain open, only the better establishments have heating, while in the bars customers tend to gather around the oven. Although Cypriot winters are mild by northern European standards, warm clothing is advisable, given the damp air. Despite the attempts of tour operators to promote the island for long winter breaks, it is, in fact, far from ideal and a more southerly destination would be preferable.

Nature and environment

With such a variety of landscape and the regional differences in climate, Cyprus is a paradise for amateur botanists. There are still areas not fully explored, and nature-lovers will make some surprising discoveries. Species unique to the island are plentiful with 110 recorded so far, including the Cyprus cotton thistle and rare orchids such as the Cyprus bee orchid *(ophrys kotschyi)*. The carob, a common species on Cyprus, is rarely found elsewhere; its close relatives died out during the Ice Age.

Prickly pear

In low-lying areas, the tall, chest-high maquis or *phrygana* is a common feature of the Cypriot landscape. Weeds, shrubs and bushes create a colourful community of plants. Against a background landscape that may well be grey and monotone, the yellow broom stands out brightly. Many herbs, such as bay, rosemary, sage, thyme, mint and marjoram, can be detected from their aroma, and the Cypriots have come to appreciate these plants for their medicinal as well as culinary properties. Walkers on the Akamas and Karpas peninsulas will be able to study the plant life in the *phrygana* more closely.

Desecration of natural features is nothing new in the modern world, but the practice can be traced back to antiquity. By the Middle Ages ore extraction and shipbuilding had reduced the woods of Cyprus to a wasteland. Voracious mountain goats nibbling away at the young saplings have also played their part, and now the woods are unable to renew themselves independently. Nevertheless, Cyprus can claim to be one of the most densely wooded islands in the Mediterranean. In the last century, large-scale afforestation was seen as a solution to soil erosion. The forestry experts have often chosen the quick-growing and undemanding Aleppo pine *(pinus brutia)* which appreciates the acid soil. This tree now constitutes about 90 percent of the island's tree stocks. Only in one or

Goat with an appetite and Aleppo Pine

Fishing out of Ayia Napa

Facing the world head on

two remote spots, such as in the 'Valley of the Cedars' have the endemic Troodos cedars *(cedrus libani ssp. brevifolia)* survived. The last moufflons *(ovis ammon orientalis)* have their homes in these woods, although visitors are unlikely to encounter these timid relatives of the modern-day sheep in the wild. They can, however, be seen in Limassol's zoo or in the Stavros tis Psokas forest station in the Paphos Forest. The moufflon appears on the island's coat-of-arms.

Turtles: Increasing pollution in the Mediterranean and the development of sandy beaches for tourism has seriously restricted the natural habitat of the sea turtle, *caretta caretta*, and the green turtle, *chelonia mydas*. Although the animals are protected species and their flesh is no longer to be found on the supermarket shelves, only one out of every 4,000 young turtles that are born will reach maturity and produce their own young. Even in northern Cyprus, there are organisations actively seeking to save these primitive armoured creatures. Signs are posted on the beaches asking the public to take due care.

Population and religion

By looking at old maps of the island's colonial past in which the original Turkish and Greek settlements are shown in different colours, it becomes clear how widely the two groups had integrated. In many towns and villages both communities lived alongside each other in harmony. After the troubles of 1963/64 the Turks withdrew into enclaves and sealed-off quarters in the towns, but following the Turkish invasion *(see page 12)* both Greeks and Turks were forced to move out into safe areas. Cyprus had undergone its own process of 'ethnic cleansing'.

Today there are only two villages in the Greek sector which have a mixed population: in Potamia, the two communities tolerate each other. In Pyla, under UN supervision, lasting feuds between the two groups continue. In the north several hundred elderly Greeks on the Karpas peninsula hold out in the face of harassment from Turkish fanatics and the authorities.

Even if anyone knows how many people live on the island of Cyprus, the politicians on both sides of the divide keep the figures a closely-guarded secret. The last 'all-island' census took place in 1960 and the statistics form an important element in discussions about the Cyprus problem, but the numbers have been extrapolated and probably over-estimated. Calculations originating in the south yield a figure of 735,000 Cypriots, 77 percent of whom are Orthodox, i.e. Greek, 18 percent are Moslem, i.e. Turkish, and the remainder are from the smaller religious communities such as Armenians, Maronites and Catholics.

Backgammon is Turkish

According to a census carried out in the northern sector in 1998, the Turkish part of the island has just over 160,000 inhabitants, not including the 35,000 Turkish soldiers stationed there. The main bone of contention is the fact that at least 60,000 Turks from the mainland have now settled on the island and the Greeks refuse to accept them as *bona fide* Turkish Cypriots. At the same time, somewhere in the region of 40,000 long-established Turks have left the island because of the depressed economic situation. If the Turkish troops stationed on the island are included, many observers calculate that the original Turkish Cypriots actually form a minority within their own sector.

Growing up in Lefkara

9

Cyprus has an ethnic problem, not a religious one. The religious ties of the native Cypriot Moslems are surprisingly weak. Anyone who takes a look inside Lefkoşa's Selimiye Mosque during Friday prayers will see that attendance is poor. On the streets, hardly any Turkish women wear the traditional headscarf. It is true that immigrants from the mainland are more deeply rooted in Islamic tradition. In their villages the otherwise rather casual observance of Ramadan, the month of fasting, is strictly enforced – it is impossible to buy even a cup of tea between sunrise and sunset.

Archbishop Makarios, president from 1960–77, was the last leader of the Cypriot Greeks to combine the spiritual and political roles. The influence of the Greek Orthodox church on politics and the everyday life of the people has subsequently diminished. Unlike Roman Catholic priests, Greek Orthodox clerics are usually married. Bishops, however, are committed to celibacy, so elevation to the higher offices within the church is in practice restricted to monks. The reverence paid to icons (*see page 79*) and the pomp of the liturgy are perhaps the most striking features of the Orthodox church.

Archbishop Makarios's tomb

Observing religious traditions

Customs

Religious traditions are still very much alive. As Cypriots of the Orthodox community are generally deeply religious, a great number of church festivals are celebrated, but their significance is rather different from what one might expect, for they feature a fascinating blend of pagan superstition and Christian rites.

Without doubt, the most important Church festival is Easter, and no expense is spared in the celebrations. Preparations begin in earnest during Passion Week. On the eve of Easter Sunday, the whole village arrives for Mass, equipped with an Easter egg and a candle. If there is no more room inside, latecomers assemble on the square in front of the church. When midnight strikes, the church door opens and the candles are lit. With the victory of Christ over death and evil, the festivities can begin. The cry '*Christos anesti!*' ('Christ is risen!') rings out, followed by the response '*Alethos anesti!*' ('Truly, He has risen!'). The Easter eggs, symbols of eternal life, are passed around and eaten, fireworks are lit, and then the congregation hurries away to continue the celebrations at home.

In the Moslem community, the circumcision ceremony welcoming the adolescent boy into the adult world is widely observed. Dressed in white, carrying a sceptre and wearing a crown, the youth is paraded through the streets like a prince, before the *sünnetçi* (circumciser) draws his knife and removes a part of the foreskin under local anaesthetic.

Economy

Over the last 30 years Cyprus has been transformed from an underdeveloped, agricultural society into a modern finance and service centre, where the standard of living

Forging ahead in Limassol

exceeds that of Greece. With continuing growth, full employment, a stable currency and negligible inflation, Cyprus would be a model of economic success within the European Union, and indeed entry into the EU is now being actively discussed in Brussels.

City Plaza in Nicosia

This economic miracle has, however, been evident only in the island's southern sector. Even before 1974 (*see Historical Highlights, page 12*), the Turks played only a minor role in the country's economic life. They were generally less well educated and the larger concerns were owned by Greeks. The boycott of northern Cyprus has closed off business opportunities on the international market. Compared with Turkey, however, northern Cyprus is still a wealthy country. Private individuals benefit from the remittances sent home by relatives in Britain and Australia and, for political reasons, the state's finances are generously supplemented from Ankara. Many Cypriots continue to hope that both parties will eventually come to appreciate the economic benefits that would accrue if the political barriers were dismantled.

Gross domestic product in the Greek sector is more than four times that of the north. Tourism plays an important part in the island's economy with over 2.1m visitors per year in the Greek south, compared with about 100,000 in the north.

11

Politics

Although the island has been split in two since 1974, in the eyes of the Greeks and according to international law the Republic of Cyprus is still undivided. Its parliament and government, made up only of Greek Cypriots, and the president, Glafkos Clerides, who is invested with wide-ranging powers, theoretically also represent Turkish Cypriots. The 'Turkish Republic of Northern Cyprus', or the 'pseudo-state' as it is scornfully described in the south, is officially recognised only by Turkey.

Guarding the Green Line

Since 1964 close on 1,000 blue-helmeted United Nations soldiers have guarded the 'Green Line' between the Turkish and Greek zones. Their function is to supervise the cease-fire and to supply those Greeks and Maronites who remained in the north with food, medicines and other goods, including televisions and bicycles. The main UN contingents are provided by the Austrian and British armies. Many Cypriots from both ethnic groups believe that the British government is not interested in a solution to the Cyprus problem, as their special status on the island would be jeopardised. Some 250sq km (100sq miles) of land around Akrotiri and Dhekelia on the southern coast of Cyprus still belongs to the UK under international law and the two British military bases there are of great strategic value.

Historical Highlights

9000–7000BC Stone tools and 'kitchen waste', excavated at Cape Gata, prove that Cyprus was inhabited during the Middle Stone Age by hunters and gatherers.

7000–3800BC In the Late Stone Age the first farms are established on the island.

3800–2500BC During the Copper Stone Age, the first tools, weapons and jewellery are produced from metal.

2500–1600BC Anatolian immigrants used to working with bronze settle on Cyprus. Towns such as Engomi and Lapithos trade with Syria, Egypt and Asia Minor. Farmers use metal ploughshares, and the worship of bulls becomes widespread.

1600–1050BC Mycenaeans colonise Cyprus and Greek culture gains a foothold. The towns build huge Cyclopean walls to defend themselves against attacks from the 'Peoples from the Sea'.

1200BC onwards Extensive Aphrodite cult in Old Paphos.

1050–500BC During the Archaic period, iron-working gains appreciably in importance. The Phoenicians, based in Kition, establish a monopoly on external trade. Persians, Assyrians and Egyptians vie for political dominance. Royal tombs are built at Salamis.

700BC Assyrian king Sargon II subjugates the city kingdoms of Cyprus.

650BC Royal Tombs at Tamassos.

540BC onwards Persian rule.

500–331BC Resistance against Persian rule preoccupies the islanders during much of the Classical period.

480BC At the Battle of Salamis, Cyprus joins the Persians against Athens.

411–374BC King Evagoras, who united the city-states from the city of Salamis, is unable to shake off the Persian yoke.

333BC Alexander the Great, with Cypriot kings' support, defeats the Persians at Issos.

331–58BC At the beginning of the Hellenistic period, the Cypriot princes acclaim Alexander the Great as their liberator. Cyprus becomes a Hellenistic cultural province.

323BC Death of Alexander the Great. Cyprus becomes embroiled in various fights to succeed him.

312BC Zeno of Citium (Kition) founds Stoicism in Athens.

294BC The island falls under the control of the Egyptian Ptolemaic dynasty.

58BC Cyprus becomes a Roman senatorial province.

50BC onwards The beginning of the long period of peace, the *Pax Romana*.

AD45/46 The apostles Paul and Barnabas arrive as missionaries and convert the Roman proconsul Sergius Paulus to Christianity in Paphos. Temples to Apollo Hylates in Salamis, Soli and Kourion are built.

AD115–116 Major Jewish uprising culminates in the expulsion of all Jews.

313 Christianity becomes the official religion of the Roman Empire.

332/342 Earthquake and famine devastate the island. Paphos and Salamis are destroyed, but Salamis is rebuilt and renamed 'Constantia'.

395 With the partition of the Roman Empire, Cyprus becomes part of the Byzantine Empire.

488 Emperor Zeno confirms the independence (*autokephalia*) of the Cypriot church.

649 Cyprus is occupied by the Arabs. By 688 it has to pay tribute to both the Byzantine Empire and the Caliphate.

730–843 The Iconoclastic Controversy rages over the use of religious images.

965–1185 Middle Byzantine Period. Cyprus flourishes. Towns include Kiti, Episkopi and Lapithos. Churches and monasteries are also founded, as well as a number of castles such as Buffavento.

1191 Richard the Lionheart conquers the island on his way to the Holy Land. He then sells it to the Knights Templar.

1192–1489 Cyprus passes to the Frankish knight, Guy de Lusignan. Catholicism becomes the state religion.

1426 The island is overrun by a marauding expedition from Egypt, and forced to pay tribute to Cairo.

1489 Caterina Cornaro, widow of the last Lusignan king, James II, bequeaths Cyprus to the Venetian Republic.

1489–1571 Venetian rule. Byzantine painting flourishes around the turn of the century.

1571 Turkish troops under Mustafa Pasha occupy Cyprus. The island becomes part of the Ottoman empire.

1660 The sublime Porte bestows the right of independent representation upon bishops.

1774 The archbishop is recognised as the representative of the Christian population.

1821 Mainland Greece's war of liberation against Ottoman rule results in massacres, and looting against the Greeks on Cyprus.

1878 The Turks lease Cyprus to Great Britain.

1914 Britain annexes Cyprus.

1930s Economic boom. Attempts are made to unify Cyprus with Greece and to liberate the island from British rule.

1950 In a referendum organised by the Orthodox Church, 96 percent of Greek Cypriots vote for union with Greece (*enosis*).

1955 EOKA's armed campaign against British installations and representatives of colonial power begins.

1960 The Republic of Cyprus is formed, with Archbishop Makarios as its first president.

1963 Makarios demands a constitutional amendment which the Turks perceive as a threat to their rights. First armed conflicts between the two ethnic groups, who begin to form enclaves.

1964 The United Nations peacekeeping force is stationed on Cyprus.

1974 Coup carried out against Makarios by the Cypriot National Guard. In July, Turkish troops invade the north of the island.

1983 Turkish Cypriots declare the north of the island the 'Turkish Republic of Northern Cyprus' but the new state is recognised only by Turkey.

1998 Negotiations on Cyprus joining the EU begin in Brussels.

Operation Attila

By the end of the 1960s the relationship between the Turks and the Greeks had improved. But this reduction in tension did not fit in with the plans of the Greek military junta. Archbishop Makarios had been seen to expose the dictators in Athens too often. So on 15 June 1974 the Athens government, supported by the National Guard, which was in Cyprus to defend the Greek community against a Turkish invasion, initiated a coup against Makarios. The action was partly intended to deflect attention from internal problems and to lead to the annexation of the island. One of the main objectives was to kill Makarios, but he avoided his pursuers by escaping through a rear exit of his burning presidential palace.

Nikos Sampson, the new leader, was held in low esteem by the Turks, who remembered his exploits during the civil war when he was known as the 'Butcher of Omorphita'. A Turkish force, far superior in numbers to the Greek National Guard, landed near Kyrenia on 20 July 1974 and the Greek adventure ended in failure as the coup leaders surrendered. The Turkish operation, code-named 'Attila', was intended to bring about the partition of the island and so the invaders withdrew to what is now the 'Green Line'. Over 6,000 Cypriots died during the coup and invasion, and a third of the population, about 200,000 people, became refugees in their own country as a process of 'ethnic cleansing' began.

Inside the Cathedral of St John

century and its interior clearly illustrates the opulent lifestyle of the upper strata of Ottoman society. The house was the residence of the dragoman (or interpreter) from 1779 to 1809. The holder of this post represented Cypriot Christians in their dealings with the Ottoman sultan and he was also responsible for collecting taxes for the Turkish rulers. His impressive possessions prove that he performed this task extremely well. On account of some intrigue, Georghakis Kornesios fell into disfavour and was beheaded in Constantinople in 1809.

19

The Archbishop's Palace

Outside the **Archbishop's Palace** ❺, built between 1956 and 1960, a huge bronze statue of Archbishop and President Makarios stands in solitary splendour. Facing him at the other end of the street is the **Monument to the War of Liberation** ❻.

The Liberation Monument

The **Cathedral of St John** ❼ (Ayios Ioannis; Monday to Saturday 9am–noon, 2–5pm) was built in 1662. Its modest exterior belies the splendour of its single-naved, barrel-vaulted interior. The iconostasis is covered with gold leaf and the colour of the 18th-century frescoes, only recently renovated, is of such a remarkable intensity that it would be easy to think that they had been completed only yesterday. Of special note is the series of pictures to the right of the bishop's throne. They show the discovery of the bones of St Barnabas and the subsequent recognition of the independence of the Cypriot church from the Byzantine emperor (*autokephalia*).

More than 150 icons from all over Cyprus are displayed in the adjacent ★ **Museum of Byzantine Art** ❼ (Monday to Friday 9am–5pm, Saturday 10am–1pm). The collection clearly illustrates the development of icon-painting from the 8th century up to the 18th century. Among the highlights of the museum are the *Lynthragomi mosaics*, which survived unscathed the attacks of the iconoclasts

Coffee break

(see page 79). A number of 15th- to 19th-century European paintings with themes from Greek Cypriot history and mythology are displayed on the upper floor. The *Bloodbath of Chios*, attributed to either Delacroix or Courbet, is among the best-known.

The nearby **Folk Art Museum ❼** (Monday to Friday 9am–5pm, Saturday 10am–1pm) is housed in one of the city's oldest buildings, part of a former Benedictine monastery dating from the 15th century. On display here are costumes, everyday objects and equipment from before the industrial era. During the Frankish period, the house belonged to the Benedictine monastery and later the Orthodox archbishop lived here.

The **Famagusta Gate ❽**, a replica of the Lazaretto Gate found in the wall at Heraklion (Crete), was the strongest section of the Venetian fortifications. The 35-m (115-ft) long barrel vaults and side chambers are now used for art exhibitions, conferences and lectures.

Also seen on the £5 note

20

The 14 rooms of the ★ **National Museum ❾** (Monday to Saturday 9am–5pm, Sunday 10am–1pm) house the finest artefacts archaeologists have discovered on Cyprus. Necklaces, small idols and items of pottery 6,000 years old from Chirokitia bear witness to the fact that even in the Stone Age man understood about art and aesthetics. One such sculptor could not resist drawing attention to human weakness with humour. In the Bronze Age clay model of a mystery ceremony, a voyeur can be seen peering over the wall of the shrine. One showcase contains a selection of the 2,000 terracotta figures – some life-size – from Ayia Irini (7th/6th century BC): warriors, priests with bull masks, minotaurs and sphinxes. Further highlights of the museum include the graceful 2-m (6-ft) high marble statue of Aphrodite of Soli and the bronze figure of the Roman emperor Septimus Severus.

The Famagusta Gate

Route 3

Tamassos landscape

Monasteries and royal tombs *See map on pages 22–3*

Nicosia – Ayios Macheras – Phikardou (50km/31 miles)

This day trip starts at the cave church of the Virgin Mary, a genuine, popular shrine, complete with superstitions. Reaching Macheras monastery requires a long drive up through pretty wooded hillsides. An impressive monument to the freedom fighter Afxentiou gives the visitor an insight into the political role of the church. For those who have made the journey here by taxi rather than hire car, the return walk through the Pedieos valley to the Herakleidos convent and the royal tombs of Tamassos will take about half a day. A drive up the long winding road to Phikardou is well worth the effort: the open-air museum reveals the travails of life in the mountains.

Rural lifestyle

The cave church of Panayia Chrysospiliotissa in **Kato Deftera** is an ancient shrine, possibly dating back to the Bronze Age when an Asia Minor mother god was worshipped here. Popular belief ascribes the four manmade caves in the steep rock face above the Pedieos to the Virgin Mary: she is said to have scraped out the rock with her fingernails after the death of Christ so that she could grieve over the loss of her son in peace. Young women who come here to pray for a happy and fertile marriage have left unusual, touching offerings. Women hoping to conceive present wax limbs or whole babies, while those waiting for the right man to come along leave wedding veils and tiaras.

The barren region surrounding ancient **Tamassos** still bears the scars left by Bronze Age miners who dug for copper here over 3,500 years ago. They cut down the wood for fuel to melt the ore and left the slag piled up in enormous heaps, where even now only a few wild plants grow. Very little of the old town has been uncovered, apart from the foundations of a temple and some workshops. Unlike the tombs at Salamis, the entrances (*dromoi*) to the **Royal Tombs** (Tuesday to Friday 9am–3pm, weekends 10am–3pm), both of which date from between 650 and 600BC, take the form of steep flights of steps. The stone roof beams, false doors, window balustrades and frieze are modelled on wooden houses, similar to those in the Near East.

Ayios Heraklidios

On the outskirts of Politiko, the **Ayios Heraklidios** monastery stands above the grave of the eponymous murdered saint. The premises were abandoned many years ago but, on the initiative of Archbishop Makarios, a community of nuns was invited to make use of the restored buildings. They have created an enchanting garden, sell delicious honey and home-made confectionery and also watch over the gilded skull of the saint, who was a companion of St Paul.

26

A narrow road winds its way through the wooded eastern foothills of the Troodos Mountains to the ★★ **Ayios Macheras** monastery (750m/2,460ft), situated in a stunning location beneath Mt Kionia. It is a popular destination for day-trippers and tourists alike, not least because of the shade and cooling breezes. The broad River Pedieos which flows sluggishly through the plain babbles cheerfully here. Outside the monastery, often shrouded in mist during the winter, a *taverna* serves lamb braised in a clay oven and also a strong *eau-de-vie*.

Ayios Macheras

A modern mosaic near the church door recounts the story of the 'Monastery of the Knife'. In the 12th century two hermits, Neophytos and Ignatios, stumbled upon a buried icon of the Virgin Mary guarded by a knife. According to another version, a dagger was actually thrust through the icon; a third, more prosaic theory suggests that the name derives from the wind which has a sharp cutting edge up here. Whatever the truth, the emperor Manuel I Comnenus (1143–80) presented the brethren with a considerable sum of money and large tracts of land to support the monastery. The early buildings have long since disappeared, as fire has ravaged the monastery on more than one occasion, most recently in 1892.

Macheras mosaic

The undisputed hero of the monastery is not, however, a devout man of the church, but a secular rebel. A small museum in the monastery remembers the exploits of the EOKA leader Grigoris Afxentiou, and a monumental bronze figure of the Cypriot hero surveys the valley. In March 1957, during the struggle for independence, he was tracked down by British soldiers to a hide-out in a cave just below the monastery. He put up bitter resistance but was killed when his pursuers, angered by the death of one of their corporals, set his refuge on fire with a flamethrower. The spot where Afxentiou died is decorated with wreaths and the Hellenistic flag, and has long been an important place of pilgrimage.

27

Walkers may take a taxi to Ayios Macheras and then enjoy a three-hour walk back down to the Heraklidios monastery on a rarely used track through the delightful Pedieos valley.

Phikardou

The lure of jobs in the towns has almost emptied the mountain village of ★ **Phikardou**, and now only a few elderly residents remain. However, it has been declared a site of historic interest, mainly for its 18th- and 19th-century rural-style houses. The owner of the village *kafenion*, Giannakos Demetris, not only welcomes visitors to this open-air museum and sells postcards, but is also the mayor, a role which is now not too demanding.

While many of the houses may look as though they have been abandoned, some are still used as barns. One or two of the dwellings have been faithfully restored, including the **House of Katsinioros** and **Achillea Dimitri**. Exhibits in this museum of rural life include old furniture, a grape press, a loom and a spinning wheel (May to August, Tuesday to Saturday 9am–1pm and 3–6pm, September to April, Monday 9am–1pm, Tuesday to Saturday 9.30am–1pm and 2–4.30pm, Sunday 9am–3pm). Ioanna Nikolaou keeps an eye on things and looks after the key.

To return to Nicosia, take the shorter and quicker route on the E904 and E903.

Barn church of Asinou

Route 4

Barn churches in the Troodos *See map on pages 22–3*

Nicosia – Limassol (180km/111 miles)

A local priest

This tour, for which a hire car is essential, includes the four main churches in Cyprus. All have been granted the coveted World Cultural Heritage status by UNESCO. Because of their overhanging roofs they have been termed 'barn churches'. The valuable paintings inside retell not just events from the Old and New Testament which are important to the Eastern church but also the lives of the saints. There are some fine walks through the Troodos woodland from all the churches, and it would be a pity to have to restrict this route to just one day. Simply asking the priest for the key can often lead to some unexpected invitations from the friendly and hospitable villagers, and time can then pass very quickly.

The chapel at ★★ **Asinou** stands in a lonely wooded spot above Nikitari, and the key may be obtained from the village priest. All the other monastery buildings which were part of the Panayia Phorviotissa (1105) have long since disappeared, and likewise nothing remains of Arsine, which was mentioned by ancient writers and from which the name of the chapel derives.

Externally, the building has an unusual structure, mainly because of the steep, double pitch roof – hence the description 'barn church'. In fact the roof is typical of Troodos churches. On closer inspection it turns out to be an outer skin, which covers the domes and the barrel vaulting, a contrivance designed to protect the **Panayia Phorviotissa** from the elements. It is possible to tell from the

Limassol as many members of Beirut's business community moved here in order to continue trading.

Unbridled growth has done little to improve the townscape. A belt of concrete, known to locals as 'The Wall', separates the town centre from the newly-built promenade. The modern shopping streets have nothing special to offer and, as a consequence of the 1584 earthquake, there are few historic buildings to see. Only the bazaar around the Greek market hall and the Palia Yitonia, the old Turkish quarter near the castle and mosque, are worth exploring. Most hotels overlook the narrow, sandy beach to the east of the town that extends for 15km (9 miles) as far as the ruins of Amathus (*see page 35*).

Limassol harbour and fisherman

History

Burial finds within the town prove that a settlement existed here in the second millennium BC, but Nemesos, as it was known in antiquity, was overshadowed by the neighbouring cities of Amathus and Kourion. As early as the 6th century, Nemesos was the seat of a bishop, but it was the Crusaders who raised the town's status. Richard the Lionheart landed here on his way to the Holy Land and while based in Limassol he conquered the whole island. In Limassol castle on 12 May 1191 he married Berengeria, whose abduction by the Cypriot potentate Isaac Comnenus had initially led to the Crusaders' invasion. In 1291 Cyprus passed to the Knights Templar who ruled from Limassol, and later the Knights of St John administered the island from here. But earthquakes, and attacks by the Genoese, Mamelukes and Ottomans brought the town to its knees. The English traveller William Turner, who visited the island in 1815, saw 150 mud huts here and described it as a 'pitiful place'. However, when the British decided to build a naval base here well over a hundred years ago, the town awoke from its slumbers.

The castle gate

Sights

Inside Limassol castle

The **Castle** ❶ (Monday to Friday 7.30am–5pm, Saturday 9am–5pm, Sunday 10am–1pm) is the only real historic site in the old town. The present building was constructed at the beginning of the 14th century over the ruins of an earlier Byzantine castle, which itself had a long and varied history. It was here that Richard I (the Lionheart) married Berengaria of Navarre and that Berengaria was subsequently crowned Queen of England by the Bishop of Evreux. From 1291 the castle served as the headquarters for the Knights Templar until this order was disbanded in 1308. King Janus handed the new citadel to the Knights of St John. In 1570, the Turks moved in and used it as a prison.

The **Cyprus Medieval Museum** is housed in the vaults where gravestones, weapons, armour and other finds are displayed. The most spectacular exhibits are the three silver plates, discovered among the famous *Lambousa Treasure* in 1902, showing scenes from the youth of King David. Large-scale photographs introduce visitors to other medieval castles and churches on the island.

34

Although the best finds from the Limassol region are kept in the National Museum in Nicosia (*see page 20*), several exhibits in the **Archaeological Museum** ❷ (Monday to Friday 7.30am–5pm, Saturday 9am–5pm, Sunday 10am–1pm) deserve special attention. These include some expressive terracotta figures kneading bread dough and a plump terracotta woman with a basket. The statue of Bes, an Egyptian-Mesopotamian god of indescribable ugliness, was excavated in Amathus in 1978.

Cyprus's only zoo

When the stands are taken down at the end of the wine festival in Limassol's **Municipal Park**, the lions, monkeys and birds in Cyprus's only **Zoo** ❸ become the town's main attraction. This is the only place where it is possible to get a close-up of moufflons, an extremely timid breed of wild sheep rarely seen in a natural setting. Some visitors to the zoo may be distressed by the inadequate conditions in which the animals are kept.

The large wine cellars and the brewery play their part in maintaining Limassol's reputation for cordiality. Based at the western end of the town on the way to the harbour,

Welcome to the brewery

some firms provide guided tours and also opportunities to sample their products. For details of the rather irregular opening times, ask in a hotel or at the tourist information office.

A narrow sandy strip in front of the hotels at the eastern end of the town is popular with watersports enthusiasts, but the Lady's Mile Beach, protected by breakwaters at the western end of the town, is better. This beach lies within the confines of the British military base and passports may be requested.

Route 6

Konos Bay, Cape Greco

The finest beaches *See map on pages 22–3*

35

Limassol – Ayia Napa – Paralimni (110km/68 miles)

Holidaymakers based in Limassol who would like to sample other (better) beaches should try those in the far south east of the island. Formerly shunned for its barren soil and sometimes mocked as the 'potato patch', after the partition the region around Ayia Napa, Protaras and Paralimni became the most important tourist region. There is no doubt that this corner of Cyprus possesses the finest beaches, but despite the fine yellow sand, it also boasts concrete hotel blocks and other architectural monstrosities. And yet there are a few idyllic spots, such as the unspoilt and windswept Cape Greco or the fishing port of Potamos. From Dherinia, it is possible to peer across the demarcation line into the ghost town of Varosha, now out of bounds even to Turkish civilians. The cultural highlights are the town of Larnaca (*see page 38*) and the Stone Age settlement of Chirokitia. A hire car will be needed for these visits.

Touring by boat

The hotel quarter in Limassol has seen unbridled growth in recent years and now extends to the edge of the Hellenistic-Roman ruins at **Amathus**. In the 19th century all the larger stones were transported to Egypt for use in the Suez Canal, and today only the foundations remain. More recently, the Temple of Aphrodite on the acropolis has been restored and now offers a photogenic backdrop as the sun sets behind the sea of houses.

Governor's Bay, whose beauty derives from the bizarrely formed, white sandstone cliffs and the tiny, secluded coves, sometimes no more than a niche in the rock, ranks as one of the finest beaches on the south coast. Basic *tavernas* offer snacks and reasonably-priced meals, but the large and well-maintained camp-site is the only place offering overnight accommodation. At the moment there are few shaded pitches.

Neolithic Chirokitia

The Neolithic settlement of ★ **Chirokitia** (winter Monday to Friday 7.30am–5pm, weekends 9am–5pm, summer Monday to Friday 7.30am–7pm, weekends 9am–5pm) lies on the hillside above the River Marinou. The walls of the round, stone huts (*tholoi*) date from the 7th millennium BC and for many years were thought to be the oldest traces of life on the island, but archaeologists at Kalavassos (Kastros) have found a village even older, and at Gata a store dates from the Middle Stone Age.

The lines of foundations are confusing. The remains of settlements centuries apart lie on top of each other. At the end of the Late Stone Age the village was abandoned, but new settlers saw the advantages of its strategic location. By 3800BC Chirokitia had been abandoned for good. Finds reflect the advances in human development. The first inhabitants lived from fishing and hunting. Only with time did they learn how to sow fields with cereals and pulses and to breed livestock. Sometimes it was immigrants from Syria and Cilicia who brought these new skills.

As for tools, sharp spear tips made from obsidian have been found, but this glassy lava rock does not occur on Cyprus, so Stone Age man in Chirokitia must have had trading links with the mainland. The way in which the round huts were built can best be seen from the *tholos* close to the entrance. Two pillars supported a wooden false ceiling and on the outside a kind of canopy surrounded the huts. Archaeologists dispute whether the reconstruction

Ayia Napa monastery

displayed in Nicosia's National Museum (*see page 20*) is accurate. The dead were buried directly beneath the house with a heavy stone laid on their chest to prevent their return. Clearly the relationship between the generations even then was not always plain sailing.

All aboard!

Once a peaceful fishing village, **Ayia Napa** promises sun and fun and is almost totally dependent on tourism. The 400-year-old **monastery** in the town centre provides a conference centre for the World Council of Churches. Its most attractive features are the Venetian fountain in the courtyard and the chapel. There is also an attendant **Folk Museum** containing examples of prehistoric threshing boards. But nobody comes to Ayia Napa for peace and quiet. Fine yellow sand, windsurfing and boat hire, riding and diving make it an ideal resort for watersports enthusiasts, while in Nissi Bay three pelicans keep the children entertained. The bars in Seferis Square are popular meeting places in the evening and the discotheques stay open until dawn.

Night lights in Ayia Napa

37

With its attractive rocky shore and inlets, **Cape Greco**, the southeastern tip of Cyprus, has recently been declared a nature conservation area. As well as many tourists, migratory birds visit the cape, pausing here before continuing their long journeys. For many of them, however, Cyprus turns out to be their last resting place as the local people cannot allow such delicacies to pass them by. The branches of the trees where the weary creatures sit are coated with birdlime and so for many of them the long trek south ends prematurely either in a Cypriot stew or on the barbecue.

Cape Greco

A 2-km (1¼-mile) walk leads round the karst rock. On foot the cape can be reached from Ayia Napa in just under two hours but sections of the path cross rough terrain. There is no proper footpath along the east coast to **Protaras** and **Pernera** either. These last two beach resorts, which have grown up during the last few years, are close to the small town of **Paralimni**.

Once water was abundant here. Creaking wind pumps, a typical feature of the region, drew the water from below ground – it was even stored in a lake during the winter – and the farmers turned the reddish brown soil into very fertile land. But intensive agriculture has caused the water table to sink ever lower and now electric pumps are required to draw the water from deep bore holes.

Dherinia has a Checkpoint Charlie atmosphere. As the last village before Famagusta, cafés and *tavernas* jockey for the best view of the 'occupied land' and the lost home of Greek Cypriot refugees.

Larnaca's old port

Route 7

★ Larnaca – boomtown behind the beach

With a population of 65,000, Larnaca is Cyprus's third-largest town and, after Limassol, is the most important port in the Greek sector. The palms beside the promenade give a hint of Nice and Cannes and Mediterranean flair, while the sandy beach is ideal for sunbathing. In the adjoining marina amateur sailors from all over the world meet and share their experiences.

Most holidaymakers fly into Larnaca, which became the island's principal airport when Nicosia was forced to close after the Turkish invasion. But Larnaca has kept a sense of normality. A walk through the former Turkish quarter around the mosque still has an Oriental feel, and the lively bazaar district near the Lazaros church makes an interesting place for a stroll. The seemingly endless sandy beach in the east of the town is overlooked mainly by hotels.

A timeless occupation

History

According to legend, Kition, as Larnaca was known in antiquity, was founded by Kittim, one of Noah's grandsons. Whether that is true or not, archaeologists have found the remains of a settlement which dates from the 2nd millennium BC. In 1075BC the town was destroyed by an earthquake, but it was rebuilt in the 8th century BC by the Phoenicians, for whom it was an important trading post. The town's most famous son is Zeno, born here in 336BC. He went on to found the Stoic school of philosophy in Athens. The Stoics believed that man should not be guided by feelings or lust but by reason. Zeno lived to old age, but then committed suicide.

The Frankish name for Larnaca was Salina, after the salt deposits, but the Genoese named it Scala or 'Port'. Today's name for the town was coined by the Venetians who during the Renaissance were interested primarily in the ancient ruins of Cyprus and gave the settlement the name Larnax (meaning 'stone sarcophagus').

Sights

The **Turkish fort** ❶ (Monday to Friday 7.30am–5pm, Thursday until 6pm), built in 1625, dominates the coastal skyline. Old cannons still stand on the huge walls. Inside, the castle displays archaeological finds from Kition and the Bronze Age settlement by the salt lake.

The **Church of Saint Lazaros** ❷ (April to August daily 8am–12.30pm and 3.30–6pm, September to March daily 8am–12.30pm and 2.30–5pm) was built by the Roman emperor Leo Vi (886–912) above the grave of the town's patron saint. According to legend, Lazarus, whom

The Church of St Lazaros

39

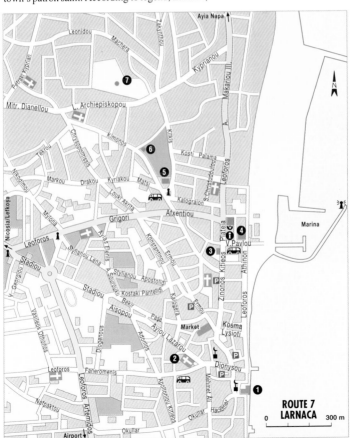

ROUTE 7
LARNACA
0   300 m

Inside St Lazaros's

Christ raised from the dead, fled to Cyprus in order to escape from the Jews of Bethany. He later became the bishop of Kition. Emperor Leo discovered his tomb in 890 and sent the remains to Constantinople. They were later removed by Crusaders who took them to Marseilles. In 1970 a tomb with a skull inside was discovered beneath the church. The skull was gilded and is on display. Visitors must decide for themselves if it ever sat on the shoulders of Lazarus. The English cemetery bears witness to that period in Cyprus's history when Larnaca was an important staging post on the trade route from Europe to Asia.

The ★ **Pierides Museum** ❸ (Monday to Friday 9am–1pm and 3–6pm, Saturday 9–1pm, summer also Sunday 10am–1pm) in Odos Zenenos Kitieos is well worth a visit. For over six generations the Pierides family collected antiquities and these are now displayed in this fine mid-18th-century house. The furnishings also give an insight into the lifestyle of wealthy Cypriots around the turn of the century. Among the highlights are the ceramics which range from the Early Stone Age to the Middle Ages.

The **Municipal Cultural Centre** ❹ (Tuesday to Friday 10am–1pm and 4–6pm, Saturday and Sunday 10am–1pm) houses a palaeontological exhibition, including skeletal remains of dinosaurs and the Cypriot dwarf hippopotamus, as well as temporary exhibitions held on a monthly basis. Devotees of ancient history may well be interested in the **Archaeological Museum** ❺, the **Acropolis** ❻ and the **excavations of ancient Kition** ❼. At the latter site, archaeologists have uncovered the foundations of Mycenaean and Phoenician temples and workshops where copper implements were made.

Beaches stretch east and west

To avoid the crowds on the town beach, try Makenzie Beach or beaches near the hotels in the west of the town.

Excursions

Hala Sultan Tekke

Few farmers now shovel salt from the salt lake in the southwest of the town, but during the winter it is visited by many migratory birds. Rising up from the bank in a well-tended garden is the minaret of the **Hala Sultan Tekke**, a mosque that is the most important place of pilgrimage for Moslem Cypriots. Hala Sultan was a relative of the prophet Mohammed who brought an Arabic army to the island in 649. According to legend, she fell from her mule, broke her neck and died here.

Apart from the Saloniki in Greece and St Catherine's Monastery on Sinai, the apse of the ★ **Panayia Angeloktistos** in **Kiti** (11km/7 miles) is the only place in the eastern church where a mosaic (6th-century) dating from before the iconoclastic era (*see page 79*) has survived. Mary, flanked by the Archangels, stands on a jewelled footstool with the Christ child in her arms.

Route 8

On the trail of Aphrodite and Apollo

Limassol – Paphos (70km/43 miles)

To make the most of this route, a car is necessary. The itinerary follows the coast to one of the Greek sector's most significant sites of antiquity. Lush citrus groves, planted only recently by Greeks evicted from Morphou, border the barren Akrotiri peninsula, and here lies the fortress of the Knights of St John at Kolossi. Situated on a plateau above the coastal plain, Roman Kourion is worth a visit, but then comes a difficult choice: whether to recover on the beach or to continue on to Aphrodite's Rock where the goddess emerged from the sea. Conclude the journey with a visit to the Sanctuary of Aphrodite at Kouklia, often mentioned in the same breath as Olympia or Delphi.

On the battlements at Kolossi

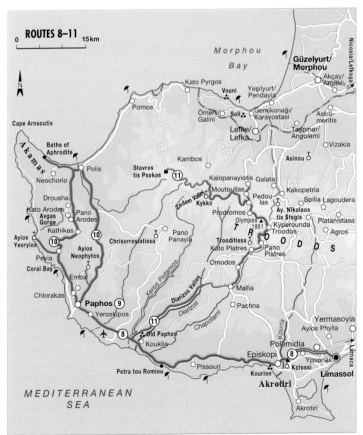

ROUTES 8–11 0 _____ 15km

Kolossi Castle

The Knights of St John's ★ **Kolossi Castle** (daily 7.30am–5pm, 7.30pm in summer) stands in a very fertile region which from the 14th century supplied Europe with sugar and a sweet dessert wine known as Commandaria. Profits only began to suffer when the Venetians were driven out by the Ottomans and competition arrived in the form of cheap sugar from the New World. Gradually the Turkish Cypriots replaced sugar cane with cotton.

Before the Knights of St John settled on Rhodes, Kolossi was for a short time the headquarters of the famous order. The defensive tower house which has survived until today was constructed in the 15th century when the knights needed to arm themselves against attacks from Mamelukes and Ottomans. Nearby stands a water-powered mill which crushed the sugar cane. Water was diverted to Kolossi from the Kouri across an aqueduct and it then tumbled 11m (35ft) downhill through a narrowing channel. Juice squeezed from the cane was probably boiled in the hall with the distinctive barrel roof. The liquid was then poured into clay vessels where the sugar crystallised into a conical mass – the sugarloaf.

Walk from the castle under the aqueduct of the old sugar mill and turn left at the next crossroads to arrive at the pilgrimage site of **Panayia Vounarkotissa**, a cave at the foot of a hill. The inside of the chapel is adorned with wax votive gifts, and in between them, as well as on the rocks next to the entrance, hang pieces of cloth, through which the devout believe that their wishes might also be fulfilled.

The ruins of ★ **Kourion** (daily 7.30am–sunset) stand on the cliff-tops against the background of an enchanting coastal landscape. After the mosaics of Paphos, these must rank as the most interesting excavations in the Greek sector of Cyprus. A tour of the site can be combined with a swim in the Mediterranean. At the foot of the cliff lies a wide, sheltered bay with grey-brown sand.

Kourion, a city founded by Achaean colonists, flourished under Ptolemaic rule but, after attacks by Arab pirates and soldiers in the 7th century, it was abandoned and the bishopric transferred to the more secure Episkopi.

A young theatregoer

The **Roman Theatre**, which had room for 3,500 spectators, has been restored and since 1963 it has staged both ancient and modern dramas. Given the fine acoustics of the sea-facing semi-circular amphitheatre, it has been used to make sound recordings. In antiquity, the theatre would have been covered by canvas and a stage wall as high as the top row of seats would have blocked the view out to sea, but over the centuries this complex of Hellenistic origins has been adapted to suit the requirements of the time. At the beginning of the 3rd century, new gangways were cut through the stand, the two front rows were removed

History

Despite the name Nea Paphos meaning New Paphos – to avoid confusion with the Shrine of Aphrodite at Paläa Paphos (Old Paphos) – the settlement here dates from ancient times. It is said to have been founded by King Agapenor after the Trojan War. Archaeologists believe that Nikokles, the last priest king of Old Paphos, built New Paphos about 320BC. With increasing numbers of pilgrims visiting the Shrine of Aphrodite, a new and larger port was thought to be necessary. Choosing the nearest point to the Egyptian port of Alexandria, the Ptolemaic rulers made New Paphos the island's administrative centre. The Roman governors also used Paphos as their capital and at that time it supported a population of some 30,000 – almost as many as live here today. The decline set in during late antiquity, but the Crusaders and Venetians still considered the town important enough for it to have a Catholic bishop. Francesco Contarini, the town's last senior cleric, was killed when Nicosia was captured by the Ottomans.

House of Dyonysos, mosaic

Sights

The **Castle ❶** (Monday to Friday 7.30am–2.30pm, Thursday also 3–6pm, weekends 10am–5pm), built by the Turks in 1592, overlooks the fishing harbour. Nearby lies a heap of stones left over from the earlier fortifications which the Venetians destroyed in 1570 as they had too few soldiers to maintain a permanent guard.

To the northwest of the harbour lay the centre of the Roman town. In 1962 a farmer ploughing his field chanced upon an ancient mosaic. Since then, archaeologists have uncovered further ★★★ **mosaics** in the vicinity and these now rank among the most significant and finest sights of historic interest in Cyprus. Even those visitors who do not find ancient ruins particularly appealing ought not to overlook these fascinating scenes from ancient mythology. The tiny coloured blocks of stone were probably made in Alexandria in the 3rd and 4th centuries and were shipped to Paphos before being assembled. They are of such beauty and so well preserved that UNESCO has justifiably acclaimed the mosaics as a World Cultural Heritage site.

The owner of the ★★ **House of Dionysos ❷** must have had a penchant for wine, as the god of wine, Dionysos, occupies a dominant position; hence the name that the archaeologists gave to this atrium villa. Liaisons illustrated on the mosaics include Pyramus and Thisbe, Zeus and Ganymede, Narcissus with his mirror image, and other couples.

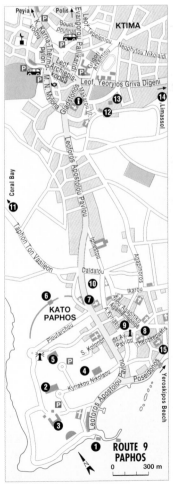

ROUTE 9
PAPHOS
0   300 m

A series of hunting scenes and geometrical patterns complete the picture.

Polish archaeologists have been responsible for excavating the ★ **House of Theseus** ❸, probably the official residence of the Roman governor. Signs of Christian influence are already evident on the mosaic showing the birth and ablutions of Achilles. The round picture in the middle depicts the heroic Theseus as victor over the slain minotaur, while beneath it a man symbolises the scene of the triumph, the labyrinth, which also appears as a geometric pattern at the margin. Above, Ariadne is shown helping Theseus to make his way out of the maze by following the woollen thread.

The three mosaics in the **House of Orpheus** ❸ (daily 9.30am–5pm, June to August until 7pm) are stylistically close to those in the Dionysos villa. Here Orpheus is charming the wild animals with his music and wrestling Hercules with a lion. The mosaics in the **House of Aion** ❸, laid after 342, show the birth, youth and triumphal procession of Dionysos. In terms of subject matter and the Baroque shapeliness of the naked bodies, they are both in the ancient tradition, but here too similarities with the life of Christ cannot be overlooked. Archaeologists are still at work in the **House of the Four Seasons**, but it is hoped that the treasures unearthed here will soon be made accessible to the public.

The fortress of **Saranda Kolones** ❹ was built by the Byzantines from the remains of ancient buildings. An earthquake in 1222 destroyed the castle shortly after it had been reinforced by the Crusaders.

The Odeon – now open to the elements

The **Odeon** ❺ can still accommodate over 1,000 spectators and it regularly stages open-air concerts and plays. Only half of the 25 rows, built on the slopes of the acropolis in the 2nd century, have been restored, but today's audiences have to do without the roof that formerly offered some protection from summer sun and winter rain.

To the northeast of the lighthouse, the visitor can stroll along the top of the old city wall. From the **City Gate** ❻ a ramp carved out of the rock leads down to the beach.

A huge turpentine tree casts its shadow over the steps to the **Catacombs of Saint Solomoni** ❼. Solomoni was forced to flee from Palestine in 168 and lived in this Hellenistic burial chamber. A spring in the base of the cave is said to cure eye complaints and anyone who ties a piece of material to the tree at the top is said to have their wish fulfilled as soon as the cloth starts to rot.

Catacombs of St Solomoni

The simple 13th-century cruciform basilica of **Ayia Kyriaki** ❽ or Ayia Chrysopolitissa as it also known, stands amid the remains of the 50 x 38m (160 x 125ft) five-naved basilica. This was clearly destroyed soon after the Crusaders arrived as they built a Gothic church nearby.

However, the place was important for both Orthodox and Western Christians on account of **St Paul's Pillar**. According to legend, when Paul came to Cyprus on his first journey, he was arrested by Jews, tied to this pillar and whipped. The *Acts of the Apostles* makes no direct reference to this incident, but does recount (13, 4–12) that Paul blinded a sorcerer in Paphos, and the proconsul Sergius Paulus, who witnessed the event, was converted to Christianity. To the north of the pillar lie the **Frankish baths** ❾, the town's old bath house.

Other graves and underground chambers were carved out beneath **Fabrica Hill** ❿, and in the Middle Ages they housed a cotton mill. Couples may be interested in **Ayios Agapetikos**, a rock chapel for lovers, sited on the hill's eastern flank. The **Digenis Rock** on the north side of the hill is the subject of a fascinating legend (*see page 77*).

The **Tomb of the Kings** ⓫ (daily 7.30am–5pm, June to August until 7pm) is situated some distance away and is best reached by taxi. Buried here in lavish vaults hewn from the rock are not, in fact, kings, but the upper strata of Ptolemaic and Roman society. With Doric pillars surrounding an inner courtyard, some of these chambers replicate the villas of the living. Amid these monuments lie some more modest catacombs and gravestones. When Christians were being persecuted, in antiquity and again during the Middle Ages, the cemetery was inhabited.

49

Professor Georgios Elliades and his wife spent their life collecting *objets d'art* and other everyday items belonging to the farmers. These treasures are now accessible to the public in the **Ethnographic Museum** ⓬ (Monday to Friday 9am–1pm and 2–5pm, June to August 4–7pm, weekends 10am–1pm), which forms a part of their home. A house chapel constructed in an ancient rock tomb is also worth investigating.

Ethnographic Museum, exhibits

Icons from the 12th–18th centuries, liturgical equipment and finely embroidered vestments are displayed in the **Byzantine Museum** ⑬ (Monday to Friday 9am–1pm and 2–5pm, June to September 4–7pm) housed in the bishop's residence.

The artefacts on show in the four rooms of the **Archaeological Museum** ⑭ (Monday to Friday 7.30am–2.30pm and 3–5pm, weekends 10am–1pm) are arranged in chronological order ranging from Early Stone Age burial offerings found in Lemba to a Renaissance baldachin. One extraordinary find is a set of clay hot-water bottles fashioned to fit the shape of male feet and hands. They were probably mass-produced for treating a Roman dignitary who had rheumatism. The town's latest attraction is the **Aquarium** ⑮ (daily 10am–8pm) which displays clourful tropical fish from all over the world.

To find a decent beach, it is necessary to go to Yeroskipou beach at the end of the promenade. Other sandy and pebble beaches on the west coast are accessible by bus.

Excursion

Yeroskipou

Yeroskipou on the road to Limassol is almost a suburb of Paphos. The name means 'Sacred Grove' and it is said that pilgrims arriving at Paphos harbour rested here on their way to the Sanctuary of Aphrodite (*see page 45*). However, little remains of this idyllic spot in a village which suffers badly from heavy through traffic.

Ayia Paraskevi inside and out

Apart from the *loukoumia*, a fruit jelly dusted with icing sugar for which Yeroskipou is famous, there are two places of interest in the town. On the platia stands ★ **Ayia Paraskevi**, one of Cyprus's oldest churches. It has the usual Greek-cross ground plan, and is surmounted by five domes. When restoration work was carried out in the interior, some simple wall paintings with geometric patterns and stylised flowers and crosses, typical of the iconoclastic period (728–843) were discovered underneath some more recent frescoes. Hence the church must have been built in the 9th century at the latest. The positioning of the Blessed Virgin in the central dome is unusual; in the Byzantine tradition of church painting, Christ as Pantokrator occupies this position.

A **Museum of Popular Art** (Monday to Saturday 7.30am–2.30pm, September to June extended 3–6pm opening on Thursdays) is situated close by. This 200-year-old house of the consular agent Hadji Smith Zymboulakis is a fine example of traditional village architecture. It contains not only the usual rural furniture and finely carved cabinets, the clothes and household objects of earlier generations, but demonstrates also the forgotten arts of domestic silk and cotton spinning and linen production.

Route 10

Ayios Neophytos monastery

The wild west *See map on page 41*

Paphos – Akamas peninsula (95km/59 miles)

The Akamas peninsula, a favourite haunt of nature-lovers, has been saved from property developers by environmental campaigners and so the turtle breeding ground at Lara beach remains undisturbed. Walkers can enjoy a day out in the Avgas Gorge and also the half-day nature trail near the 'Baths of Aphrodite'. The little town of Polis is popular with young independent travellers as it is the only place in Cyprus where overnight accommodation is available in small pensions or cheap private rooms. Anyone looking for a lively nightlife in Polis is in the wrong place. The full tour is best undertaken in a hire car, but it is suitable for cyclists as long as they are not afraid of a few steep hills. Walkers will have to use taxis to reach the more remote sights as buses only operate between Paphos and Polis.

Ancient texts at Ayios Neophytos

First stop is ★ **Ayios Neophytos monastery** (April to September daily 9am–1pm and 2–6pm, winter daily 9am–4pm). The story goes that St Neophytos, who had a love of travel, had been robbed of his money in Paphos in 1159 while en route to Palestine. Impoverished, he saw his plight as a sign from God and decided to stay put. The spot he chose for his enclosure (*enkleistra*) and where he was to spend the next 65 years was by a spring at the entrance to a wooded valley.

Using only simple tools Neophytos took a whole year to cut a cave out of the sheer rock face above the present monastery. In 1170, at the request of the Bishop of Paphos, he accepted a number of pupils but he found himself ill-

At the altar
Neophytos's cells

suited to life in a monastery. So the recluse dug out a second cave a little higher up and cut a shaft through to the first cave so that he could follow the liturgy in the first cave without having to make contact with his fellow monks. Finally he dug his own grave in the rock, but his last wish – to be left to rest in peace until the Last Judgement – has not been fulfilled as his bones and skull, covered in silver and now a shade of yellow from the countless kisses of his followers, are displayed in the 15th-century monastery church.

Even during his lifetime, the walls of **Neophytos's cell**, smoothed with a layer of plaster, were covered with splendid paintings. Two of the scenes show Neophytos himself. In one he is being carried up to heaven by angels and in the other he is kneeling at the feet of Christ, flanked by John and Mary. In the **monastery church**, there are three clear styles. In the ascetic-style frescoes on the west wall, the saint, clad only in sack-like drapes, seems sullen and weary. The pictures in the apse of the chapel are quite different: the figures here display refinement and elegance but they were the work of artists from the imperial court in Constantinople. The most recent pictures, such as the foot-washing scene, were added during restoration work in 1503 and the style has a more popular appeal.

Visitors to Ayios Neophytos should also look inside the new **museum**. At weekends or on 28 September, St Neophytos's Day, the monastery is transformed into a busy market and it is difficult to imagine that once a hermit communed with God and nature here. For a hermit, however, Neophytos played an extraordinarily active part in the island's politics. Apart from a wealth of religious writings, he penned a chronicle entitled *Regarding the Misfortune of Cyprus*, a detailed account of the Crusaders' conquest of the island.

For a long time ★ **Polis** (pop 2,000) has been popular with young holidaymakers who have made their own way to Cyprus. There are no hotel complexes and visitors can stay in small pensions or private rooms rented out by locals. However, even in Polis Chrysochou, the 'Town with the Golden Sand' as it is officially known, a few villas and apartment blocks have been built and the attractive main square and the street leading to the pedestrianised zone have been smartened up. In antiquity, the town of Marion was situated a little nearer the sea and the copper mined in the hinterland was exported from the harbour. At the end of the last century, archaeologists uncovered a number of tombs from Marion's golden age; however, these have been filled in and are awaiting another round of excavations. The shingle beach, interspersed with sandy sections, extends for miles as far as the Baths of Aphrodite.

Only a few tracks and bridle paths cross the uninhabited ★ **Akamas peninsula**. This northeastern tip of Cyprus has survived as a habitat for rare plants and strongly-flavoured wild herbs such as sage and thyme. The British army, which occasionally uses the Akamas for artillery practice, and Cypriot environmental campaigners are to be thanked for saving the peninsula from tourist development. As yet, the government's promise formally to declare the region a national park has not yet been honoured. Consequently, there is little that can be done legally to curtail the activities of the four-wheel-drive enthusiasts and motor-cyclists who chase through the woodland.

Peaceful Akamas

53

If exercises are planned, a red flag will be hoisted at the start of the footpath and warning lights switched on. Another danger comes from unexploded shells which can sometimes be found lying in the grass. Do not touch them but notify the forest rangers or the restaurant staff.

A road leads from Polis past the fishing and holiday village of **Lachi** to the **Potamos** estate, ending at a car park outside a large restaurant. Continue on foot and before long the path reaches ★ **Loutra tis Aphroditis** (Baths of Aphrodite), hidden away in a fertile grove. According to legend, the goddess and her lover Akamas sought privacy here. Refreshingly cool water trickles from a rocky ledge into three natural basins. Bathing in the pool is said to bring beauty and eternal youth, and anyone who drinks the spring water will soon fall head over heels in love. Two ★ **nature trails** follow Aphrodite's footsteps further into the peninsula's interior. The couple are said to have rested at **Pyrgos tis Rigaenis**, a ruined monastery in the shade of some primeval oaks. Another tale links the place with Queen Regina and Digenis the Giant (*see page 77*).

Loutra tis Aphroditis

Exterior and interior
of Ayios Georgios

Taking life easy

The villages near **Drousha** in the **Laona** region are trying, with the support of money from the European Union, to create a 'gentler form of tourism'. The village school by the church square in Kathikas has been converted into a cultural centre, where slides provide information on the everyday life of the local farmers, fauna and flora and possible walks. The road from Drousha to **Neochorio** via the abandoned Turkish village of **Androlikou** is little used by traffic and so features in many of the walking tours organised on Cyprus.

The pilgrims' church of **Ayios Georgios** at **Cape Drepano** overlooks a fishing harbour and a small beach. The foundations and mosaics of a basilica provide evidence that in late antiquity an important town once stood on the plateau, but little is known of its fate. The inhabitants buried their dead in rock tombs near the steps to the quay. Archaeologists hope that the excavation work underway on the tiny offshore island of Geronissos will reveal more about the mysterious town that probably dates from the Ptolemaic era.

The quiet village – not much more than three *tavernas* – comes alive on Saturdays. Baptisms take place in the church and that is always an excuse for Cypriots to organise a lavish feast. Presents, votive offerings and wax figures of babies can be bought at the **market**. The faithful then offer them to the church saint. Single people still in search of a partner may find that the wishing tree outside the **Byzantine church** will help to bring them love. But if they have no faith in the practice of tying rags to the tree trunk, then a candle in the church might do the trick: say the name of the loved one three times and then turn the candle upside down. If it continues to burn, love and happiness will follow.

To the north of Ayios Georgios, a coastal path runs beside a turtle beach. In order to avoid crushing any of the eggs which are buried, under no circumstance must cars be driven by the water's edge during June and August. One of the finest walks in western Cyprus runs through the ★★ **Avgas Gorge**. Only at midday does the sun penetrate to the floor of this steep and narrow ravine. In places the path is the stream fed by rock springs, but there is no cause for alarm: the water is not only shallow, but also cool and refreshing. The path ends in a hollow with sides so steep that even the goats find it difficult to negotiate. Anyone planning a day's walk to Arodhes would be well advised to join a guided walking party.

Coral Bay, a booming holiday village, marks the return to civilisation. Corallina Bay, on the other side of the **Maa peninsula** (where there was a Bronze Age settlement), is popular with windsurfers.

Route 12

★ Girne/Kyrenia – Cyprus's picture-book harbour

The idyllic harbour set against the steeply rising Beşpar-mak (Five Finger) mountain range makes Girne, called Kyrenia by the Greeks, into one of the most attractive resorts on the island. In the bay, shaped like a horseshoe and dominated on the eastern side by a sturdy castle, fishing boats rock gently alongside fashionable yachts whose owners, at least during the summer season, probably prefer this sleepy but attractive little town to the busy marinas of the Aegean. In days gone by, the warehouses around the harbour were used to store locally-produced carob and olive oil. Only a few have been converted into hotels and holiday apartments, while behind lie the ordinary homes of the local people. The promenade belongs to pedestrians – no cars disturb the peaceful atmosphere of souvenir shops, café terraces and *tavernas*.

The old harbour and home with the catch

History

It is thought that Girne/Kyrenia was first settled in the 10th century BC by Greek Achaeans, but little is known about the town until it came under the control of King Nikokreon of Salamis (312BC). Although a castle and walls were built in the 8th or 9th century, the town was attacked and plun-

59

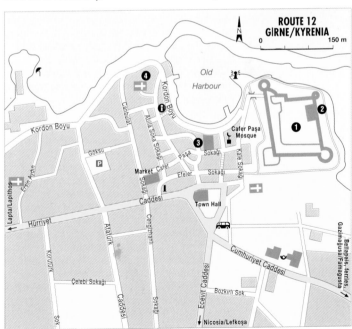

ROUTE 12
GİRNE/KYRENIA
0   150 m

dered by Arabs and pirates on a number of occasions. In 1192 the town and the family of the last Byzantine ruler fell into the hands of the Crusaders. Four centuries later, in 1570, the town and castle were captured by the Ottomans without a struggle. At the beginning of this century many British officers, enticed by the mild climate, came to Kyrenia either as tourists or to retire. For an idea of the atmosphere in northern Cyprus during the unsettled 1950s, read Lawrence Durrell's *Bitter Lemons*. The English writer lived for several years in Bellapais.

Sights

Harbour fortress

The **Castle ❶** at Girne (daily 8am–1pm and 2.30–5pm; closed at weekends in the winter), built in the 8th century by the Byzantines, is the best preserved harbour fortress on the island. The base of the round tower has survived from the earliest days and marks the northwest corner of the complex. At that time the Byzantine **St George's chapel** was located outside the castle. The Lusignans renovated the north and east and built the horseshoe-shaped **Northeast Tower** and also the living quarters in the inner courtyard – adding a touch of courtly elegance to military functionalism.

In the 16th century the Venetians modified the castle still further; they are responsible for its present design. In 1374 Genoese siege engines inflicted considerable damage to the walls and after the development of siege cannons, the fortress with its high, but rather weak walls, was too vulnerable to defend. Apart from the new **Northwest Tower**, there was no space for further reinforcement on the seaward side. But as a maritime power with galleys controlling the seas, the Venetian strategists mostly feared attacks from the land, so a new wall was constructed and the intervening land filled with earth and stones, thus creating a rampart 38m (125ft) thick. An impression of the strength of these fortifications can be gained from the long, slippery passageway which leads through them down into the casemates of the **Southwest Bastion**. The strengthened fort was never put to the test, though. In 1570 and without a shot being fired, the Venetian troops – demoralised by the fall of Nicosia – surrendered to the Ottoman admiral Sadîk Paşa, who still guards over the entrance from his **sarcophagus** in the gatehouse.

Living from the sea

The **Shipwreck Museum ❷** (daily 8am–1pm and 2.30–5pm; closed at weekends in the winter), on the east side of the castle courtyard, houses the hull of a sailing ship that sank or was scuppered by pirates some time between 288 and 262BC. At least four sailors went down with their ship and its cargo. Finds include the mariners' cutlery, amphoras filled with almonds and 26 mill stones, probably used as ballast.

The minaret of **Cafer Paşa Mosque** and two date palms tower above the roofs of the houses, making a picturesque sight when framed against the mountain backdrop. A small **Folk Art Museum**  (Monday to Friday 8am–1pm, key at the entrance to the castle) is accommodated in an old warehouse by the harbour and is well worth a visit.

Completed in 1860, the dazzlingly white **Church of the Archangel Michael** ❹ is, after the harbour and castle, the third symbol of Girne/Kyrenia's past. A **collection of icons** (Monday to Friday, 8am–1pm and 2.30–5pm, on an irregular basis in winter) awaits the visitor in what is, apart from the iconostasis, a plain interior. Sadly, these exhibits, collected from churches in the surrounding villages, are poorly labelled.

As there are no beaches in Girne/Kyrenia, follow the coast road to the east.

Excursions

For its position alone ★★ **St Hilarion** (daily 8am–5pm) must rank as one of the finest sights in northern Cyprus. This marvellous castle of battlements and towers seems to grow naturally out of the steep limestone rocks of the Beşparmak mountains.

Its name probably originates from a Palestinian monk who spent his twilight years in Cyprus (c. 370), but the annals of sainthood contain 15 other pious men bearing the same name. A monastery emerged from the original settlement and then the Byzantines extended it into a castle in the 10th century. From 1228–32 Hilarion played a key role in Emperor Friedrich II's attempt to seize Cyprus, almost in passing, while on his way to the Holy Land during the 6th Crusade. Those loyal to the emperor and the supporters of the Lusignans exchanged the roles of besieger and besieged several times, until the emperor's army was eventually annihilated on the pass below the castle.

St Hilarion

Hilarion consists of three clearly defined wards one above the other on the side of the hill. The stables and the soldiers' quarters are at the lowest level; above them are the old monastery and refectory in which the Lusignans held their banquets. The climb to the upper ward of the badly decaying castle is hard work but, once there, the view over the coastal plain and out to sea will repay the effort. The best time to view the whole complex is early in the morning when the sun is in the right position for photographers.

In the rectory of Bellapais

The Gothic ★★ **Bellapais Abbey** ('Abbey of Peace', daily 8am–5pm, 7pm in summer) stands in the heart of a sleepy village of the same name. Alongside the abbey stands the 'Tree of Idleness', made famous by Lawrence Durrell in his book *Bitter Lemons*. It is indeed a good place to take a rest. Augustinian monks founded a monastery here in 1205 and they were soon joined by monks from a Premonstratensian order. The abbey's pointed arches and ribbed vaulting in northern French Gothic style ought to have looked out of place in this Levantine landscape but, surprisingly, it seems to blend in well with the olive groves, cypresses and date palms. The Lusignan coat-of-arms above the entrance to the dining hall serves as a reminder of Bellapais's royal benefactors: when Jerusalem fell, the Augustinians were expelled from the Holy Land and Hugo I donated extensive estates to the order. To the great anger of the archbishop, Hugo III (1267–84) granted the abbot the right to wear a bishop's mitre during services. By the time the Ottomans arrived, Bellapais was both structurally and morally disintegrating. A Venetian inspector who visited the site in the mid-15th century complained that the monks were not reading Mass, devoting themselves instead to their concubines and their children.

62

Bellapais Abbey cloisters

Route 13

Forgotten sights by Güzelyurt/Morphou Bay

Girne/Kyrenia – Soli – Vouni (85km/53 miles)

A hire car is essential for this day trip (*see page 93*). The itinerary starts by following the beaches along the north coast and then on to the citrus groves around the little country town of Güzelyurt ('beautiful country') to the Turks or Morphou to the Greeks. In the spring when the orange and citrus trees are in blossom, a delightful aroma spreads over the fertile plain. Below Soli, a town that grew rich from the copper deposits, the ore-processing and loading equipment quietly rusts away to create a modern industrial ruin. Archaeologists continue to ponder over who built Vouni Palace on the table mountain above the coast. Certainly none of the ancient writers mention it.

The town of **Karmi/Karaman** was discovered initially by the British and many have second homes or have retired here. As many of the property owners stay for only a few weeks each year, their houses are often let as holiday homes. Ask locally for more information. Perhaps it was the presence of so many outsiders in the village that saved the outwardly rather unassuming church from damage during the Turkish invasion. The icons and iconostasis can be viewed late on Sunday mornings.

Thanks to the plentiful water supply from local springs, the region around **Lapta** has enjoyed the benefits of fertile soil, a factor which attracted settlers as long ago as the Late Stone Age. The ancient city-state of Lapithos was situated near Alsancak beach, where the Turks landed on 20 July 1974. A concrete memorial marks the spot. Over a hundred years ago (on land now belonging to the military and not open to the public) near Acheiropitos monastery, farmers discovered a fine set of early Christian silver tableware. Some pieces from the buried treasure which had been hidden by the Arabs are now displayed in the National Museum in Nicosia (*see page 20*).

Güzelyurt – famous for its fruit

Güzelyurt/Morphou with its 12,000 inhabitants is situated in the middle of a huge citrus plantation. The fruit is packed or processed in the town's factories and sent for export. Until 1974 Morphou was largely Greek; many of the present residents originated from the former Turkish wine-producing villages in the Troodos. The 18th-century church of ★ **Ayios Mamas** includes fragments from ancient structures. Under a Gothic arch, where panels recount the life story of the saint, lies the tomb of Ayios Mamas. The iconostasis with its painstakingly carved

leafwork and the fighting mythical beast is a testimony to the craftsmanship of the Venetian period. Mamas can be seen on many of the icons and also as a relief on the west portal – where he is shown as a combination of shepherd and hermit – riding a lion with a lamb on his arm.

As well as a protector of animals, Mamas is also revered as the patron saint of tax dodgers. According to folklore, one day Mamas was summoned to Nicosia to appear before the governor to explain why he had not paid any taxes. On the way, Mamas tamed a lion which was on the point of killing a lamb and rode off to the capital on its back. When the governor of Nicosia heard the news, he cancelled the meeting and it is said that the tax collectors never troubled Mamas again.

A local veteran

The key to the church is kept, as it always has been, in the episcopal palace, although now it is a natural history and archaeological museum (Monday to Friday 8am–1pm and 2.30–5pm). Its most famous exhibit is a statue of the multi-breasted goddess of fertility, Artemis of Ephesus, found in Salamis in 1980. A pair of golden ear-rings and some quaint terracotta lamps from the Hellenistic era are on display in the same room.

Gemikonaği, or the 'ships' resting place' is now a truly restful place but it has not always been so. Abandoned slag heaps, rusting silos and a conveyor belt projecting out to sea bear witness to the fact that the town's harbour was once used for exporting copper ore. Mining started in antiquity and continued until the 1960s when it ceased to be profitable.

Solitary Soli: the theatre

The ancient city of ★★ **Soli** was founded in 600BC, when King Philokypros summoned the famous Athenian statesman and poet Solon to Cyprus and named the new city after him. As a result of its copper mining in-

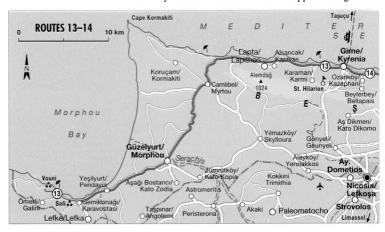

ROUTES 13–14

0   10 km

Cape Kormakiti

M E D I T E R R A N E

Taşucu

Girne/Kyrenia

Lapta/Lapithos   Alsancak/Karavas

Koruçam/Kormakiti

Alemdağ   Karaman/Karmi

Ozanköy/Kazaphani

Çamlıbel/Myrtou   1024   St. Hilarion

Beylerbey/Bellapais

B   Ş

Morphou   E   Aş Dikmen/Kato Dikomo

Bay   Yılmazköy/Skylloura

Güzelyurt/Morphou   Serachis   Gönyeli/Geunyeli

Zümrütköy/Kato Kopia   Alayköy/Yerolakkos   Ay. Dometios

Vouni   Yeşilyurt/Pendayia   Aşağı Bostancı/Kato Zodia   Kokkini Trimithia   Nicosia/Lefkoşa

Ömerli/Galini   Soli   Gemikonağı/Karavostasi   Astromeritis   Strovolos

Lefke/Lefka   Taşpınar/Ahgolemi   Peristerona   Akaki   Paleometocho   Limassol

dustry, the city-state quickly flourished, but it was sacked by the Persians in AD498 and then ravaged by the Arabs 150 years later. The British completed the job by carrying off much of the stone to help build the Suez Canal.

Soli is noted for the 'Aphrodite of Soli', unearthed by Swedish archaeologists over 60 years ago. This highly stylised statue has been used by the marketing department of the tourist board as a symbol for ancient Cyprus. Although the 2nd-century BC artefact occupies a place of honour in Nicosia's National Museum (*see page 20*), it is now recognised to have been mass-produced by an unknown workshop. The rebuilt **Roman theatre** is worth seeking out. Not only does the auditorium have superb acoustics, but the seats offer a fine view out over the meadows and gardens as far as the horizon, where sea and sky merge in a haze. Mosaics on the floor of the **basilica** portray animals, including a fine swan. An inscription pleads, 'O Christ, save the person who donated this mosaic' but perhaps someone should plead for the mosaic as it is completely unprotected, facing exposure both to the elements and the footsteps of irresponsible visitors. Perhaps it is a blessing that only a fraction of the old town has been uncovered. The Canadian team working on the site had to end their project in 1974 for political reasons.

Floor mosaic in the basilica

On the road to Vouni

65

Between 498 and 449BC the ★ **Palace of Vouni**, on a hill 235m (770ft) above sea level, was the residence of the Persian governor, who no longer felt safe in Soli and considered the inhabitants rather hostile. The bathing complex, consisting of steam bath, caldarium and frigidarium, was technically on a par with the baths the Romans built centuries later. Only the foundations of the palace remain because it was destroyed by fire in the 4th century; however, the atmosphere and view make a visit worthwhile.

The Palace of Vouni

Route 14

From coast to coast *See map on pages 64–5*

Girne/Kyrenia – Five Finger mountains – Gazimağusa/
Famagusta (160km/100 miles)

Five Finger mountain

Like the pointed crest of a dragon, the Five Finger mountains (Turkish = Beşparmak, Greek = Pentadaktylos) ex-
tend from Cape Korucam along the north coast and across
the island as far as the Karpas peninsula. Where the rocks
are at their steepest, Buffavento castle clings to a rugged
mountain top almost 1,000m (3,250ft) above sea level.
The abandoned Antiphonitis and Sourp Magar monasteries
lie hidden away in the woods, and the wide range of
Cyprus's flora is catalogued in the herbarium at the
Alevkaya forest station. The Mesoaria plain on the southern flank of the mountain range contains little of interest. Anyone coming from Girne/Kyrenia and not wishing
to go on to Gazimağusa/Famagusta can miss out the second half of this route. To complete this route in a day, a car
is essential, although the little used forest tracks in the
mountains are ideal for walkers and mountain bikers.

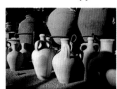

Pottery for sale

Start out on the good but narrow and winding coast road
from Girne/Kyrenia, passing the **Acapulco**, **Lara** and
Alakatï beaches. A kilometre (¾ mile) before the junction
to Karaağaç, explorers with a good sense of direction (follow the fragments of pottery) can investigate the ruins
of the old port of **Charcha** which lies between the road
and the sea. What looks at first sight to be an idyllic bay
turns out on closer inspection to be awash with plastic
débris and other rubbish. The prevailing north wind means
that refuse tipped into the Mediterranean in Turkey floats
south on to the beaches of Cyprus.

Above **Esentepe** in a dense mixed forest lies the monastery
of ★ **Antiphonitis**, or the 'echo' monastery, so-called because of its position in a hollow. The last 500m (1,600ft)
of the steep descent are best covered on foot. A superb
liquiambar styraciflua, whose resin was used by the monks
to make incense, marks the entrance to the monastery. It
stands in a clearing, which in early spring is carpeted with
red poppies.

Antiphonitis is Cyprus's last Byzantine monastery
(12th-century) where the dome does not rest on four but
on eight supports. While it is true that the chapel on Mount
Hilarion is of the eight-pillar type, the dome there has col-
lapsed. Many of the frescoes have been destroyed, often
as a result of art thieves. The Archangel Michael, for example, in the late Comnene apse was badly damaged when

Turkish attackers to advance. His grave forms the centrepiece of a small **museum** where the exhibits document the history of the town. Outside the entrance lie memorial tombs to the victims of the civil war. Photographers will appreciate the view over the old town.

Canbulat museum: tomb inscription

The district of **Varosha** with its fine beach and more than 80 hotels was once the jewel in Cyprus's tourist industry but since 1974 it has been a ghost town. It borders the demarcation line and is now controlled by Turkish forces. Fearing a protracted and bloody battle over the properties in this largely Greek quarter, the invading army did not originally impose an occupying force. They only entered once it was clear that the residents had all fled in panic. As a bargaining counter in negotiations, Varosha is closed even to Turkish Cypriots.

Only the northernmost tip of Varosha beach near the Palm Beach Hotel is accessible. Other good beaches can be found by the ruins of Salamis and the hotels nearby.

Excursions

Visitors to the excavations of **Engomi** near the village of Tuzla will need a good imagination or else training as archaeologists. The foundations of Cyprus's first settlement and an important centre of the copper industry dating from 2000BC are nothing more than a jumble of stone walls. Even what is thought to be the **grave of Nikokreon**, the last king of Salamis, who preferred to cast himself into the flames of his burning palace than to give himself up to Ptolemaios, is from a layman's point of view simply a mound of earth at the western exit of Tuzla.

Icon in St Barnabas's

Of more interest is the **monastery of St Barnabas**. Outsize paintings on the walls of the monastery church (1756) recount the story of the founding of the Cypriot Orthodox church. In 478, guided by a vision, Archbishop Anthemios discovered the grave of Barnabas. As the church

Weavers at work in the monastery

could therefore be traced back to an apostle, it was entitled to demand independence (*autokephalia*) from the other Orthodox patriarchs. An **Archaeological Museum** (daily 8am–1pm and 2–5pm) in the former monastery displays a selection of finds made after 1974, including some superb terracotta votive offerings.

The road to Salamis passes close to the **royal necropolis** where rulers and nobles were buried between the 8th and 6th centuries BC. Although all the 150 known graves were plundered both in antiquity and during the Middle Ages, a number of burial offerings have survived. Jewellery, clay vessels and furniture are displayed in Nicosia's National Museum (*see page 20*). Horses drew the funeral bier to the tomb, were killed and then buried alongside their royal masters. Their skeletons have been preserved and can be seen under glass. Early Christians covered the **Prison of St Catherine** (tomb no. 50) with barrel vaulting. The princess who converted to Christianity is said to have been incarcerated here by her family. The chapel has been on the itinerary of pilgrims to the Holy Land since the late Middle Ages.

According to legend, ★★ **Salamis** (daily 8am–5pm, in summer until 6pm) was founded by Teukros, a Trojan warrior mentioned in Homer's *Iliad*. He named the city

The skeleton of a horse

Salamis

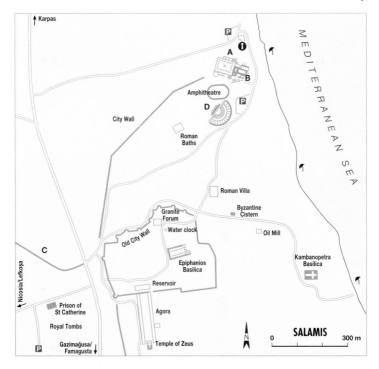

↑ Karpas

MEDITERRANEAN SEA

P

A

B

Amphitheatre

D

P

City Wall

Roman Baths

Roman Villa

Byzantine Cistern

Granite Forum

Water clock

Oil Mill

Old City Wall

C

Epiphanios Basilica

Kambanopetra Basilica

Reservoir

← Nicosia/Lefkoşa

Prison of St Catherine

Agora

Royal Tombs

Gazimağusa/ Famagusta ↓

Temple of Zeus

P

N

SALAMIS

0   300 m

after his birthplace, an island to the south of Athens. In the 10th century BC Salamis took over from the abandoned Engomi as an important trading centre. At its peak as many as 120,000 people lived in Cyprus's biggest town, but under the Romans it ceded its leading role to Paphos. In the 7th century AD, Salamis was finally abandoned and the inhabitants moved to Famagusta. It had been badly hit by an earthquake, had suffered a number of attacks by Arabs and the harbour had silted up.

Only a fraction of the town has been excavated. With the exception of one older tomb, the buildings date from the Hellenistic and Roman eras. Allow plenty of time for a full visit. Although Cyprus's largest open-air museum covers a wide area and can be glimpsed from a car, it is best to visit the ruins on foot. Try to end up at the beach near the ruined site where acacias, eucalyptus trees and pines provide ample shade for a picnic. In spring the blossom is stunning. Visitors in a hurry will probably have to restrict their tour to the following highlights.

The **Roman gymnasium [A]** was built above an older Hellenistic wrestling school but, with its courtyard surrounded by a shaded colonnade, it was more than just a centre for sporting activities. The menfolk would meet here to discuss politics and philosophy and to conduct their business rather as in a modern coffee house. However, as with all public buildings, only an elite sector of the community, i.e. those with Roman citizenship, were allowed access. The statues, the finest of which are on display in Nicosia's National Museum (*see page 20*), were all beheaded. The culprits were probably early Christians who saw the statues as symbols of paganism, but Venetian souvenir hunters are also suspected.

73

A good head shorter

Directly adjacent to the eastern colonnade are the **baths [B]**. The remains of mosaics showing scenes from Greek mythology can be seen in the niches of the sudatorium (sweating room) to the southeast. With the advent of Christianity or at the latest during the iconoclastic period, the niches were bricked up to conceal the pagan pictures from the eyes of guests. Water for the baths and the rest of the town arrived via an **aqueduct [C]**, traces of which are still visible at the junction with the road to the royal necropolis. Kythrea, about 60km (37 miles) away, was the source of the town's water.

To reach the Roman **theatre [D]** pass the stadium and the remains of an arena. With space for between 15,000 and 20,000 spectators, the theatre was one of the biggest in the Mediterranean. In antiquity a Dionysos altar would have stood in the middle of the semi-circular orchestra. Twenty of the 50 rows have been restored and, during the summer, plays and folk music performances are occasionally held here.

The Roman theatre and local guides

Route 16

The Karpas peninsula

Gazimağusa/Famagusta – Monastery of Andrew the
Apostle (130km/80 miles)

Isolated beach on the peninsula

The isolated beaches of the Karpas peninsula form one
of the last coastal areas where turtles can still lay their eggs
without being disturbed. On early summer nights – as long
as they are not disturbed by light or noise – the 250kg
(550lb) females crawl ashore, dig out a hole in the sand
and lay about 40 tennis-ball-sized eggs. Provided the eggs
are not discovered by foxes, unearthed by children building sandcastles or destroyed by car tyres, after about two
months the baby turtles will emerge from their eggs, push
their way out of the sand and hurry towards the water. (Cars
should be kept off the sand from June onwards to avoid
harming the turtle eggs – *see page 8*).

On the route itself, ruined churches and mosaics testify
to a lively past. In one or two villages that the road passes
through, an ageing minority, probably no more than a
few hundred Greeks, refused to join the exodus to the south
in 1974 and stayed put; most of the inhabitants, however,
are now Turks from the mainland. Tourers hiring a car
from Gazimağusa/Famagusta should plan for at least one
overnight stop in Dipkarpaz.

74

Freshly caught fish

In **Iskele**, formerly Trikomo, the cruciform **Panayia
Theotokos** basilica has been converted into an icon museum (Monday to Saturday 8.30am–1pm and 2.30–5pm).
Of most interest are the 12th-century, courtly-style frescoes, showing scenes from the Resurrection of Christ,
which can be admired in the south dome and by the arch
in front of the apse.

It is hard to resist the sandy beach lined with sunbeds
and parasols near the quay in the fishing village of **Boğaz**.
The restaurants here specialise in serving freshly-caught

Early Christian art

During the years of rule from Byzantium, sacred images were systematically destroyed through the fervour generated by the Iconoclasm (746–843), when religious fanatics strictly interpreted the Third Commandment (Thou shalt not make unto thee a graven image ...). Consequently, few early Christian mosaics have survived in the Eastern church. One remains at Kiti near Larnaca and another, the Mosaic of Lynthragomi (Karpas), is on display in the Byzantine Museum in Nicosia. This was illegally exported to the USA in 1974 but has now been returned.

Many of the early Christian churches were destroyed by Arab invaders, but there are ruins, such as at Kourion and Salamis, which are worth investigating.

Byzantine churches and Orthodox painting

Cyprus is a treasure trove of Byzantine art. There are few countries in the Orthodox Christian world where so many masterpieces of Byzantine art – from the 11th to the 18th centuries – can be found within such a small area. One architectural curiosity, which is only found in Cyprus, is the 'barn church' of which there are several examples in the Troodos mountains (*see pages 55–8*). From the 13th century these cruciform churches in Byzantine style were covered with a weatherboard roof for extra protection against the winter snows.

Byzantine barn church and fresco

The interiors of many Greek Orthodox churches are richly decorated with icons and frescoes, and those on Cyprus are no exception. To many westerners the rigid and formal execution seems odd but, to understand about icons in the Orthodox church, it is necessary to examine their

Interior of St John the Evangelist

function. Unlike western sacred art which aims to represent biblical scenes in a totally realistic way, Greek Orthodox art seeks to create a supernatural, mythical dimension in which the past, present and divine somehow merge with one another. In this way, the stories recounted in the Bible cease to be unique events and acquire a timeless character.

By idealising concepts of the eternal and the sublime, the saint on the icon becomes ever-present. Just how difficult it is to express spiritual concepts using worldly forms was demonstrated by the response of the iconoclasts, the Greek Orthodox fundamentalists who set out to destroy icons and religious images (AD726–843). These opponents of icons saw it as blasphemy to portray Christ and the apostles figuratively, but the icon painters solved the problem by establishing a set of commonly understood formulae and symbols which allowed little room for individual expression.

The most important models, passed down through the generations, are the 'acheiropoeita', the pictures of Christ that were 'not painted by human hand'. These include the cloth that bore Christ's facial imprint. The icons which the evangelist Luke is said to have painted were also part of the repertoire because Luke saw Jesus and Mary face to face and was a witness to many of the events described in the New Testament.

Fresco painting also has its own set rules in the Orthodox Church, with Jesus the *Pantocrator* (Almighty) occupying pride of place in the dome, the prophets in the drum, the apostles in the pendentives, and so on. It is important to differentiate between the elegant, courtly style and the ascetic approach of the monks, both of which were subject to the increasing suppression of the Orthodox church by the Roman church via Catholic crusaders.

Pantocrator in the dome

Western and Turkish influences

Grand Gothic churches were built under the Lusignans. The Venetians and the Genoese who followed built huge fortifications to protect the towns from invasion by the Turks. The painting of murals continued to flourish in the Orthodox churches, and from about 1500, the influence of the Italian Renaissance becomes evident. But with the Ottoman conquest of Cyprus, practically every type of religious art ceased with the exception of icon painting. Churches were converted into mosques but none of the spaciousness of Seljuk and Ottoman architecture found its way on to the island. The Moslems simply added a minaret to the church, marked the direction of Mecca by a *mihrab* and removed all Christian imagery and decorations. Very few new mosques were built during the Turkish era, although caravanserais and fortifications were constructed.

Sinan Paşa Mosque, the former Church of St Peter and Paul

Shopping and souvenirs

Shopping in Cyprus follows the European practice, so haggling over marked prices is not normally acceptable.

Traditional souvenirs from **southern Cyprus** are the colourful woven goods and Lefkara lace. Clay pottery and engraved copper vessels or brass plates are also reasonably priced. *Soujoukko*, strings of nuts dipped in grape juice, are popular with youngsters, as are *glyko*, fruit soaked in syrup, while *commandaria*, a sweet wine, is often appreciated by older people. The Handicraft Centres run by the Ministry of Trade and Industry are good places to see the full range of locally-produced crafts.

Portable souvenirs

Popular souvenirs available in **northern Cyprus** include embroidery, carpets *(kelim)* and wickerwork (made from grasses or reeds). Leather goods are often good value, (but always check the quality of the sewing) and gold jewellery is also relatively cheap.

Postal services

In northern Cyprus the best advice is to enquire at a post office or in a hotel as the cost of postage has increased several times in a year because of currency devaluations. Northern Cyprus is not a member of the Universal Postal Union and so all mail to foreign destinations has to pass through Turkey. Do not write Cyprus on any mail to northern Cyprus as it will arrive in southern Cyprus and not be forwarded. Instead of 'Cyprus', write 'Mersin 10, Turkey'.

Telephone

Calls may be made from telephone offices or telephone booths but not from post offices. Telephone connections to northern Cyprus are made via Turkey: dial the Turkish dialling code 0090, followed by 392 (the dialling code covering the whole of northern Cyprus), then the number of the party you wish to reach.

Southern Cyprus

Coin-operated public telephones (2, 5, 10, 20 cent coins) are gradually being replaced by call boxes which only accept phone cards. Telephone offices, post offices and banks sell telephone cards worth C£2, C£5 and C£10.

Dialling prefixes: Ayia Napa, Paralimni 03; Larnaca 04; Limassol 05; Nicosia 02; Paphos, Polis 06.

Northern Cyprus

It is possible to make international calls from all coin-operated phone boxes. Tokens must first be bought from the post office or other shops with the 'jeton bulunur' sign. Few phones accept phone cards. No dialling prefix is necessary when phoning within northern Cyprus.

Time

Cyprus is two hours ahead of GMT. In summer the clocks run one hour ahead.

Electricity

Electricity is supplied at 220–240V AC. Generally, electrical outlets correspond to British standards.

Units of measure

British visitors will be familiar with miles, pints and gallons, but they will find *oka* (2¾lbs) used at the market and *dönüm* (2¼ acres) as a unit of area.

Nudism and topless sunbathing

Pretty well anything goes on the beaches in the Greek sector as long as a small patch of material covers the private parts. In Cyprus nobody goes into the water totally naked, at least not where others can watch. On beaches used by local people, women do not go topless.

In the Turkish sector, the rules are much stricter and topless bathing is only acceptable on the hotel beaches.

Phrenaros Church, Ayia Napa

Churches and monasteries

When visiting churches, monasteries or mosques, both men and women should cover their shoulders and knees. In some of the monasteries that receive a large number of visitors, the staff will issue shawls or cloaks if necessary. It is considered offensive for visitors to turn their back on an iconostasis. The room behind it is reserved for the priest and only men are permitted to enter. If a church has been opened specially, a small donation or the purchase of a candle is expected. Kissing icons would be regarded as excessive.

Photography

Taking photographs and using video cameras in state-owned museums is allowed only with a special permit, but it is generally acceptable to take photographs at archaeological sites, with the exception of one or two new digs, where details of all the finds have not yet been publicised. Taking photographs of and filming the area around the Green Line, other military installations and soldiers is strictly forbidden.

Language

English is widely understood in Cyprus.

Tipping

A 10 percent tip on top of a restaurant bill is normal, while taxi drivers look forward to receiving a rounded up amount for the fare. Room staff in hotels also expect a small tip.

Newspapers

Foreign newspapers usually arrive in Cyprus with a delay of one or two days and can be obtained from kiosks in the main resorts and in Nicosia. The *Cyprus Mail* and the *Cyprus Weekly* are English-language papers.

Selling yesterday's news

Medical assistance

Many Cypriot doctors are trained in Britain and therefore speak English. Normal consulting times are Monday to Friday 9am–1pm and 4–7pm. Details of the night-time emergency service and which doctors are on call at the weekend are given in the daily newspapers and in southern Cyprus by phoning 192.

Good private insurance is advisable and will provide for every eventuality. Consultations with doctors, hospital fees and medicines have to be paid for at once.

Handicapped

The Pancyprian Organisation for Disabled Persons, 50 Pendelis Street, Dasopolis, PO Box 4620, Nicosia, tel: 02 426301, can assist disabled travellers.

Emergencies

Dial 199 in **southern Cyprus** for police, fire brigade and first aid.

In **northern Cyprus** there is no single number to cover all the emergency services. Police station numbers are: Lefkoşa/Nicosia, 228 3311; Gazimağusa/Famagusta, 815 2125; Girne/Kyrenia, 815 2125; Güzelyurt/Morphou, 714 2140; Dipkarpaz, 372 2344.

Heed the fire warnings

Forest fires

During the dry season, Cyprus is plagued by forest fires. Discarded cigarette ends or the careless use of barbecues often turn out to be the cause. Please take care, especially when signs show high fire risks. On the Troodos mountain range there is an emergency forest telephone to notify the forest rangers of any fires.

Diplomatic representation

UK: High Commission, Alexander Pallis Street, Nicosia, tel: 02 473131.
USA: Embassy, Dositheos and Therissos Street, Lycavitos, Nicosia, tel: 02 465151.

As northern Cyprus is not internationally recognised, there is no official diplomatic representation. In serious emergencies, the United Nations peacekeeping mission (UNFICYP; tel: 227 3006) may be persuaded to mediate on behalf of Western European consulates.

Accommodation

The boom in hotel construction continues apace in the south and new, good quality hotels open every year. In the north the range of accommodation is limited, with most of the hotels dating from before partition.

In the Greek sector

Modern development, Ayia Napa

For a long time Ayia Napa/Paralimni and Limassol saw the bulk of the new holiday development, but in recent years Paphos has emerged as the tourists' favourite resort. Few hotel beds will be found in Nicosia, Polis and the Troodos. All hotels, holiday apartments and campsites are regulated by the tourist board (*see pages 94–5*), who will be happy to send a list of accommodation available.

Hotels are categorised according to a one- to five-star system. Overnight tariffs as laid down by the authorities are displayed in all rooms. In the low season from November to Easter (May in the mountains), most hotels will negotiate a reduction.

Self-catering accommodation ranges from smart villas by the sea to simple flats in urban apartment blocks. The advantage of this kind of accommodation, of course, is having access to a cooker, which obviates the need to go out for every meal. Visitors are advised to book such accommodation through a reputable travel company. Because of government regulations, accommodation in private rooms is hard to come by. Ayia Napa is one exception. Here, younger travellers with limited budgets can find reasonably-priced rooms.

Youth hostels exist in Nicosia, Larnaca, Paphos and Troodos. For further details or group bookings contact: Cyprus Youth Hostel Association, 34 Th. Theodotou, Nicosia, tel: 02 442027, fax: 02 442896.

The **campsites** by the coast have plenty of space even in high season. Camping is popular with Cypriots, but in summer they opt for the mountains rather than the seaside. The Troodos campsite, situated in pine woods, is a good place to make contact with the locals. The forestry authorities in the mountains permit walkers to camp at the official picnic sites, where basic facilities are provided.

In the Turkish sector

Hotels and **villas** in the Turkish sector are also classified according to a star system, but the hoteliers themselves award the stars and are often rather generous when assessing their own establishment. Travelling independently in northern Cyprus is probably cheaper than arranging rooms through a travel agent.

The hotel complexes on the east coast (in and around Famagusta) overlook miles of sandy beaches, but the flat hinterland is not so attractive. Girne/Kyrenia is a different matter. As the mountains are within easy reach, there are plenty of opportunities for walks, but the beaches do not compare with those on the east coast. On the Karpas peninsula tourists will find beds in rather basic hostels.

Self-catering accommodation is restricted to the north coast around Girne/Kyrenia. Of the rather limited choice, the holiday villas and apartments in Karmi, an idyllic village on the slopes of the Beşparmak mountains, are by far the best. Private rooms are not normally available.

Proper **campsites** are located near Gazimağusa/Famagusta and Girne/Kyrenia. *Camping sauvage* is permitted and the Cypriots in the north derive the same pleasure as their southern counterparts from pitching their tents at the picnic sites in the Beşparmak mountains. Visitors should be aware of the dangers that exist near the military installations and prohibited zones.

Hotel selection

The following are hotel suggestions for some of the most popular spots, listed according to three categories: $$$ = expensive; $$ = moderate; $ = cheap

A tasteful complex in the north

Acapulco Bay (Northern Cyprus)
$$Club Acapulco, tel: 824 4450, fax: 834 4455. Holiday village with an attractive garden and its own beach.

Agros (area code 05)
$$Rodon Hotel, tel: 521201, fax: 521235. A new hotel on the edge of the town with swimming pool and garden. Half-board only in high season.

Ayia Napa (area code 03)
$$$Nissi Beach, 3km (2 miles) from the town centre by Nissi Bay, tel: 721021, fax: 721623. Large garden, own watersports centre, freshwater swimming pool, tennis courts. Disco and night-club are situated well away from the bedrooms and do not disturb guests. **$$Cornelia**, 23 Makarios Avenue, tel: 721406. Central location.

High season in Ayia Napa

Boğaz (Northern Cyprus)
$$Cyprus Gardens, tel: 371 2722, fax: 371 2559. Villas set in a lush garden, swimming pool, own beach, tennis courts, riding stables and bike hire. **$$View**, tel: 371 2651, fax: 228 2603. Smart new hotel located in a commanding position, 10 minutes' walk from the harbour.

Drousha (area code 06)
$$Drousha, tel: 332351, fax: 332353. On the edge of the village. Fine views and rustic furnishings. Self-catering apartments.

Old Famagusta

The Dome Hotel

Gazimağosa/Famagusta (Northern Cyprus)

$$$Palm Beach, tel: 366 2000, fax: 366 1200. Northern Cyprus's top hotel lies 20 minutes' walk from the town centre, by the beach close to the Varosha barrier. **$Altun Tabya**, Kïzïl Kule 9, tel: 366 3404. A family-run concern in a quiet part of the old town. Fourteen simply furnished rooms with shower/WC and balcony. More hotels, all pre-dating 1974, are located about 10km (7 miles) to the north by Salamis beach.

Gemikonağı/Karavostasi (Northern Cyprus)

$$Soli Inn, tel: 727 7695, fax: 727 7575. Best hotel in the region, with pool and restaurant.

Kakopetria (area code 02)

$$Linos Inn, tel 923161, fax: 923181. Hotel in a renovated house in the centre of the village.

Girne/Kyrenia (Northern Cyprus)

$$$Dome, Kordon Boyu, west of the old harbour, tel: 815 2453, fax: 815 2772. An older hotel with spacious rooms. In a central location on a rocky peninsula. **$British Hotel** (formerly Ergenekon), Eftal Akta Cad., by the old customs house, tel: 815 2240, fax: 815 2742. A popular hotel, some rooms with harbour view.

Larnaca (area code 04)

$$$Golden Bay, Dhekelia Road, 10km (7 miles) along the coast to the east, tel: 645444, fax: 645451. The best hotel in the town, with freshwater swimming pool, sauna and private beach. **$Sandbeach Castle**, Piale Pasha, tel: 655437, fax: 659804. A family-run hotel with unusual architectural design. By Makenzie beach.

Lefkara (area code 04)

$Pano Lefkara, tel/fax: 342000. Hotel furnished in traditional style. Reservation advisable.

Limassol (area code 05)

$$Curium Palace, 2 Byron, tel: 363131, fax: 359293. 1970s urban hotel near the Archaeological Museum, small garden with swimming pool. **$Continental**, 137 Spyrou Araouzou, tel: 362530, 362534, fax: 373030. Basic, older-style hotel with a popular café on the promenade.

Nicosia (Greek sector) (area code 02)

$$$Holiday Inn, 70 Regaena, tel: 475131, fax: 473337. Best hotel in the old town. Fine view from the roof terrace (with swimming pool). **$Averof**, tel: 463447, fax: 463411. In a quiet residential area to the west, 15 minutes' walk from the town centre. Furnished in country style.